D1065113

THE CHINESE HOROSCOPES LIBRARY

RAT

KWOK MAN-HO

DORLING KINDERSLEY
LONDON • NEW YORK • STUTTGART

DK

A DORLING KINDERSLEY BOOK

Senior Editor	Sharon Lucas
Art Editor	Camilla Fox
Managing Editor	Krystyna Mayer
Managing Art Editor	Derek Coombes
DTP Designer	Doug Miller
Production Controller	Antony Heller
US Editor	Laaren Brown

Artworks: Danuta Mayer 4, 8, 11, 17, 27, 29, 31, 33, 35;
Giuliano Fornari 21; Jane Thomson; Sarah Ponder.

Special Photography by Steve Gorton. Thank you to The British Museum, Chinese Post Office,
The Powell-Cotton Museum, and The Board of Trustees of the Victoria & Albert Museum.

Additional Photography: Martin Brigdale, Eric Crichton, Michael Crockett, Steve Gorton,
Dave King, Colin Walton.

Picture Credits: Bridgeman Art Library/Oriental Museum, Durham University 18tl & r;
Sport Parachutist 23br.

First American Edition, 1994
2 4 6 8 10 9 7 5 3

Published in the United States by Dorling Kindersley Publishing, Inc., 95 Madison Avenue,
New York, New York 10016

Copyright © 1994
Dorling Kindersley Limited, London
Text copyright © 1994 ICOREC

All rights reserved under International and Pan-American Copyright Conventions. No part
of this publication may be reproduced, stored in a retrieval system, or transmitted in any
form or by any means, electronic, mechanical, photocopying, recording, or otherwise,
without the prior written permission of the copyright owner. Published in Great Britain by
Dorling Kindersley Limited.
Distributed by Houghton Mifflin Company, Boston.

ISBN 1-56458-608-1
Library of Congress Catalog Number 93-48006

Reproduced by GRB Editrice, Verona, Italy
Printed and bound in Hong Kong by Imago

CONTENTS

INTRODUCING CHINESE HOROSCOPES

For thousands of years, the Chinese have used their astrology and religion to establish a harmony between people and the world around them.

The exact origins of the twelve animals of Chinese astrology – the Rat, Ox, Tiger, Rabbit, Dragon, Snake, Horse, Ram, Monkey, Rooster, Dog, and Pig – remain a mystery. Nevertheless, these animals are important in Chinese astrology. They are much more than general signposts to the year and to the possible good or bad times ahead for us all. The twelve animals of Chinese astrology are considered to be a reflection of the Universe itself.

YIN AND YANG

The many differences in our natures, moods, health, and fortunes reflect the wider changes within the Universe. The Chinese believe that

YIN AND YANG SYMBOL
White represents the female force of yin, and black represents the masculine force of yang.

every single thing in the Universe is held in balance by the dynamic, cosmic forces of yin and yang. Yin is feminine, watery, and cool; the force of the Moon and the rain. Yang is masculine, solid, and hot; the force of the Sun and the Earth. According to ancient Chinese belief, the concentrated essences of yin and yang became the four seasons, and the scattered essences of yin and yang became the myriad creatures that are found on Earth.

The twelve animals of Chinese astrology are all associated with either yin or yang. The forces of yin rise as Winter approaches. These forces decline with the warmth of Spring, when yang begins to assert itself. Even in the course of a normal day, yin and yang are at work, constantly changing and balancing. These forces also naturally rise and fall within us all.

Everyone has their own internal balance of yin and yang. This affects our tempers, ambitions, and health. We also respond to the changes of weather, to the environment, and to the people who surround us.

THE FIVE ELEMENTS

All that we can touch, taste, or see is divided into five basic types or elements – wood, fire, earth, gold, and water. Everything in the Universe can be linked to one of these elements.

For example, the element water is linked to the Rat and to the Pig. This element is also linked to the color black, salty-tasting food, the season of Winter, and the emotion of fear. The activity of these various elements indicates the fortune that may befall us.

AN INDIVIDUAL DISCOVERY

Chinese astrology can help you balance your yin and yang. It can also tell you which element you are, and the colors, tastes, parts of the body, or emotions that are linked to your particular sign. Your fortune can be prophesied according to the year, month, day, and hour in which you were born. You can identify the type of people to whom you are attracted, and the career that will suit your character. You can understand your changes of mood, your reactions to other places and to other people. In essence, you can start to discover what makes you an individual.

DIVINATION STICKS
Another ancient and popular method of Chinese fortune-telling is using special divination sticks to obtain a specific reading from prediction books.

CASTING YOUR HOROSCOPE

*The Chinese calendar is based on the movement of the
Moon, unlike the calendar used in the Western world,
which is based on the movement of the Sun.*

Before you begin to cast your
Chinese horoscope, check your year
of birth on the chart on pages 44 to
45. Check particularly carefully if
you were born in the early months of
the year. The Chinese year does not
usually begin until January or
February, and you might belong to
the previous Chinese year. For
example, if you were born in 1961
you might assume that you were
born in the Year of the Ox.
However, if your birthday falls
before February 15 you belong to the
previous Chinese year, which is the
Year of the Rat.

THE SIXTY-YEAR CYCLE

The Chinese measure the passing of
time by cycles of sixty years. The
twelve astrological animals appear
five times during the sixty-year
cycle, and they appear in a slightly
different form every time. For
example, if you were born in 1948

you are a Rat in the Warehouse, but
if you were born in 1972, you are a
Rat on the Mountain.

MONTHS, DAYS, AND HOURS

The twelve lunar months of the
Chinese calendar do not correspond
exactly with the twelve Western
calendar months. This is because
Chinese months are lunar, whereas
Western months are solar. Chinese
months are normally twenty-nine to
thirty days long, and every three to
four years an extra month is added to
keep approximately in step with the
Western year.

One Chinese hour is equal to two
Western hours, and the twelve
Chinese hours correspond to the
twelve animal signs.

The year, month, day, and hour
of birth are the keys to Chinese
astrology. Once you know them,
you can start to unlock your personal
Chinese horoscope.

Water		
Earth		Gold
Wood		Yin
Fire		Yang

CHINESE ASTROLOGICAL WHEEL
In the center of the wheel is the yin and yang symbol. It is surrounded by the Chinese astrological character linked to each animal. The band of color indicates your element, and the outer ring reveals whether you are yin or yang.

· RAT ·
MYTHS AND LEGENDS

The Jade Emperor, heaven's ruler, asked to see the Earth's twelve most interesting animals. When they arrived, he was impressed by the Rat's cleverness, and awarded it first place.

In China, the Rat is associated with money, and when its scrambling feet are heard at night it is said to be "counting money."

THE RAT'S WEDDING DAY

The Wah Chiu family lived long ago in China. It was a normal and peaceful house until one night, when the father of the family heard strange noises coming from a room that had been firmly locked for years. Bravely unlocking the door, he peered in and saw an amazing sight – a traditional marriage procession of rats, dressed in fine robes.

Over the next few nights, he returned to watch, in secret, as the rats went through all the Chinese wedding ceremonies. At first, he did not tell his family of his discovery, for fear that they would question his sanity. One night, however, he invited them to come and watch. The old room lay silent and still, and as he suspected, his family began to question his sanity.

A few days later, a Taoist priest came by. He looked up at the house and said to the father, "This house has an evil spirit in it. With the

RAT ON A VINE
This exquisitely carved rat is virtually concealed among the leaves and fruit of a vine. It is turquoise and dates from China's Ch'ing dynasty.

help of the household god, I can defeat it." The father was delighted, and invited the priest into the house. The priest summoned six spirits from the walls and killed them. As he left he said, "Make sure you leave out food and drink to thank the household god."

The father was very surprised indeed, because household gods do not usually require thanks in the form of food and drink. He therefore ignored the priest's warning.

The very next day the house was overrun by rats, and the father realized what had happened. The priest had in fact been an evil spirit sent by the rats to get food for their celebrations. Within days, the rats had invaded every corner, and had driven the family out.

Luckily, a real Taoist priest heard about the Wah Chiu's troubles and came with powerful magic to deal with the rats. Within a few days, every rat was dead. The story spread far and wide, and the Chinese realized that rats need proper care. Consequently, even now, a day is set aside as the Rat's Wedding Day. Each year, every household in China leaves out food and drink, and goes to bed early, allowing the rats to marry in peace.

LEGENDARY SNUFF
Chinese legend says that the Rat tricked the cat out of meeting the Jade Emperor. Their enmity can be seen on this ancient Chinese snuff bottle.

· RAT ·
PERSONALITY

The Rat is a gregarious, intelligent, and polite creature. It has an ever-widening circle of acquaintances, but rarely lowers its guard to form deep friendships.

You are seemingly carefree and patient, but underneath this façade is a wary, critical character. You take your own sincerity and friendships very seriously. If you find yourself deceived or ignored in any way, you are quick to take a suitable form of revenge.

MOTIVATION
The possibility of excitement is always a motivating force in your life, and you are spurred on by the appeal of new opportunities and adventures.

The risks that you seek are not necessarily physical or dangerous, but you do need your intellect and imagination to be stretched. You are bored by everyday practicalities and are frustrated with predictable situations. The antidote to this numbing sense of tedium is usually leaping into action at unexpected moments and relishing the exhilaration of being a law unto yourself.

RODENT BUCKLE
This Chinese rat- or mouse-shaped jade buckle is from the Ch'ing dynasty.

THE INNER RAT
You are an excellent performer. You shine in social situations and always maintain a comfortable, warm atmosphere. However, during this process, you rarely reveal your real self, and your defenses remain intact. Your privacy is jealously guarded,

and your independence is fierce. You relish peace and solitude, and you are also possessive. There is a personal price to pay, however: your natural watchfulness makes you high-strung and easily overwrought.

Anyone who attempts to enter your life uninvited runs the risk of being wounded by your sharp tongue. Essentially, however, you want to make connections and form relationships with other people.

Although this may seem unlikely after you have responded with such prickliness to the initial intrusion, this is simply your tried and trusted method of self-protection. Once you have allowed your barriers to be broken down, you make an attentive and exciting friend.

As a romantic partner, you are imaginative and passionate, but you must always be reassured that your love is requited.

CHINESE WATER DROPPER
This remarkable, ratlike porcelain creature is decorated with a piece of vine on its side. It was used as a water dropper and was made in the K'ang-hsi period (1662–1722) of the Ch'ing dynasty.

PARENTHOOD
You are naturally enthusiastic as a parent and are always ready to encourage your children's hobbies. The more unusual your children's interests, the more you will enjoy taking part in them.

THE RAT CHILD
The young Rat is likely to demand a taste of freedom from an early age. Careful nurturing of the Rat child will stimulate its natural curiosity and give it a strong sense of emotional security.

· RAT ·
LOVE

The Rat is capable of great passion when it feels that it is truly understood by its partner. In a committed relationship, it is attentive, caring, and faithful.

In the excitement and passion of a new relationship, you tend to be easily swept away and to exist in a highly charged emotional state.

When you are in love, you are always alert, and your feelings are ever changeable. You are capable of great acts of generosity, but if you find yourself deceived or disappointed, you are quick to retaliate.

Ideally, you are suited to the Dragon and to the Monkey. The Dragon's charm and confidence will complement your enthusiasm and attentiveness, and, in spite of regular arguments, you are likely to have a long, successful relationship.

The Monkey is also a good match for you, but you must not allow it to dominate. Love with another Rat will be powerful and potentially tempestuous, but be careful that the relationship does not quickly burn itself out. Although your passionate nature may not be entirely satisfied by the Ox, you should enjoy its independence and reliability.

GODDESS OF LOVE
Kuan Yin is a powerful figure in Chinese mythology. Once a male Buddhist deity, she is now known as the goddess of mercy, and as Sung-tzu, the giver of children.

CHINESE COMPATIBILITY WHEEL

Find your animal sign, then look for the animals that share its background color – the Rat has a pink background and is most compatible with the Dragon and the Monkey. The symbol in the center of the wheel represents double happiness.

A relationship with the Snake, Dog, Pig, or Tiger may be happy, but probably not perfect. The Snake and the Tiger could be difficult to control; the Dog may seem lacking in vitality; and the Pig is likely to be too innocent for you.

In a relationship with a Horse, you will both fling yourselves into the romance of the situation. You, however, can still remain critical, but the Horse is

ORCHID

In China, the orchid, or Lan Hua, is an emblem of love and beauty. It is also a fertility symbol and represents many offspring.

likely to stay naive. The Horse could easily become too involved and lose its sense of judgment.

A relationship with the Rabbit will have to be based on trust and a firm friendship. You are unlikely to find happiness with the Ram – you will be frustrated by its dreamy, creative nature, and it will be hurt by your harsh criticisms. Your critical nature may find its match in the Rooster, but there is a danger that you will criticize each other throughout the relationship.

· RAT ·
CAREER

The Rat's independent, persistent, and wary character is best suited to small-scale enterprises, where it will not feel puzzled or threatened by other people.

MUSICIAN
Discipline is just as important as talent for the aspiring musician, and the Rat has an abundance of both qualities. The challenge of learning to play the Chinese musical stone or the Chinese flute requires persistence, and should appeal to the Rat.

Chinese jade musical stone

Chinese jade flute

Books

LITERARY PURSUITS
The Rat is intelligent and astute, and enjoys the rigor of intellectual work. The maverick, independent life of a publisher, writer, or literary critic could suit its personality, as well as stretch its intellect.

STOREKEEPER

Although the Rat is more of an intellectual than a manual worker, it can derive great satisfaction from owning and running a store. A small-scale business, such as a gourmet shop, could give it an arena in which it is able to express itself. Even more importantly, it would be its own boss and would not be threatened by other people's hidden agendas.

Grocer's scales

High-quality groceries

Toiletry bag

TRAVELING SALESPERSON

Blessed with an innate sense of survival, the Rat likes working on its own. It would enjoy being a traveling salesperson, since this would allow it to make its own decisions and take responsibility for its actions.

Suitcase

· RAT ·
HEALTH

Yin and yang are in a continual state of flux within the body. Good health is dependent upon the balance of yin and yang being constantly harmonious.

There is a natural minimum and maximum level of yin and yang in the human body. The body's energy is known as ch'i and is a yang force. The movement of ch'i in the human body is complemented by the movement of blood, which is a yin force. The very slightest displacement of the balance of yin or yang in the body can lead to poor health.

However, yang illness can be cured by yin treatment, and yin illness can be cured by yang treatment. Everybody has their own individual balance of yin and yang. It is likely that a hot-tempered person will have strong yang forces, and that a peaceful person will have strong yin forces. Your nature is identified with your health, and before Chinese medicine can be prescribed, your moods have to be carefully taken into account. A balance of joy, anger, sadness, happiness, worry, pensiveness, and fear must be maintained. This fine balance is known in China as the Harmony of the Seven Sentiments.

LINGCHIH FUNGUS
The fungus shown in this detail from a Ch'ing dynasty bowl is the "immortal" lingchih fungus, which symbolizes longevity.

REHMANNIA GLUTINOSA
The sweet-tasting root of Rehmannia glutinosa is often prescribed to restore balance to the blood.

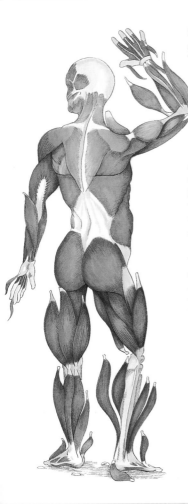

Born in the Year of the Rat, you are associated with the element water. This element is linked with the kidneys, bladder, bones, and ears.

These are the parts of the body that are relevant to the pattern of your health. You are also associated with the emotion of fear and with salty-tasting food.

The herb *Rehmannia glutinosa* is associated with your Chinese astrological sign. It is mixed with figwort to control high body temperature, and prepared with Chinese yam and wolfberry to ease diabetic thirst.

R. glutinosa is a main ingredient in the Eight Precious Soup, which treats anxiety, depression, and loss of appetite. *R. glutinosa* is also used in the extremely powerful Increase of Dew Soup.

Chinese medicine is highly specific; therefore, never be tempted to take *R. glutinosa* or any other herb unless you are following professional advice from a fully qualified Chinese or Western doctor.

ASTROLOGY AND ANATOMY

Your element, water, is particularly associated with the urinary tract. The kidneys are considered to be yin, and the bladder is believed to be yang.

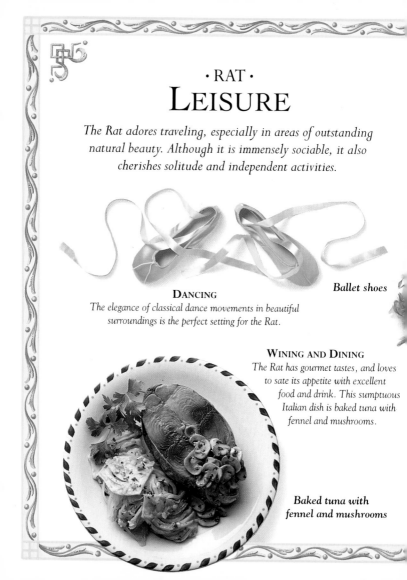

· RAT ·
LEISURE

The Rat adores traveling, especially in areas of outstanding natural beauty. Although it is immensely sociable, it also cherishes solitude and independent activities.

Ballet shoes

DANCING
The elegance of classical dance movements in beautiful surroundings is the perfect setting for the Rat.

WINING AND DINING
The Rat has gourmet tastes, and loves to sate its appetite with excellent food and drink. This sumptuous Italian dish is baked tuna with fennel and mushrooms.

Baked tuna with fennel and mushrooms

Fake tiara

Opera glasses

PERFORMING ARTS
Opera, or any performing
art, is particularly
appealing to the
flamboyant Rat. It
loves to show off and
parade its talents,
especially when it can
wear a disguise.

Feather boa

Open parachute

PARACHUTING
Although the Rat is
essentially a gregarious
character, it also seeks quality
time alone. Pandering to its
dynamic nature, the Rat loves
adventures and would be exhilarated by
a daring activity such as parachuting.

· RAT ·
SYMBOLISM

Each astrological animal is linked with a certain food, direction, color, emotion, association, and symbol. The Rat is also associated with the season of Winter.

Chinese jade rat

COLOR
In China, black is the color of honor. It is also the color that is linked with the Rat. This black jade rat is from China's Han dynasty (206BC–220AD).

FOOD
There are five tastes according to Chinese astrology – salty, acrid, bitter, sour, and sweet. Salty foods are associated with the Rat.

Grains of salt

Antique Chinese compass

DIRECTION
The Chinese compass points south, whereas the Western compass points north. The Rat's direction is the north.

Set of scales

SYMBOL
The Rat's symbol in Chinese astrology is the scale.

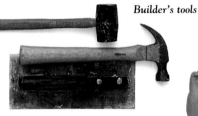

Builder's tools

ASSOCIATION
Tools used in building, such as a hammer, mallet, and level, are linked with the Rat.

Fearful baby

EMOTION
The Rat is connected with the emotion of fear.

RAT ON THE ROOF

~ 1924 1984 ~

*As your name suggests, you are a highly conspicuous Rat.
You always tend to expose yourself to risk, and you run the
danger of being spotted and chased.*

You are linked to Spring. This indicates that throughout most of your life you are likely to be as frisky as the young in Spring. Sometimes you tend to act without due thought or consideration and allow yourself to be ruled by your emotions.

Your energies will invariably draw many people to you, but your inability to control these energies, as well as your temper, may hurt people, too.

You are associated with a young bud bursting with life, and also with midnight. These associations combine to make you an extremely thrusting personality who is always likely to be brimming over with energy. But do try to be careful – the Rat's innate tenacity can be a strength or a weakness. In a Rat on the Roof, it runs the risk of being a weakness because you simply refuse to recognize when you are wrong.

PERSONALITY
Any Rat born in these years is likely to be impatient, and will not be able to suffer fools gladly. Completing a task probably does not interest you in the slightest – just like a lover in Spring, your mind is never likely to be focused on one area of your life for long.

All Rats possess a natural sense of cunning, but in a Rat on the Roof, this characteristic can lead to inner tensions. These will leave you susceptible to illness and accidents. Sometimes you may even take unwise risks and disregard sensible warnings. You are always likely to suffer as a result, so do try to curb these impulses.

FEMALE CHARACTERISTICS
A female Rat on the Roof should be able to exert a certain degree of control over her disruptive inner

Rat on the Roof

energies, due to the calming and soothing influences of the yin force. Her life is likely to be stable, enjoyable, and successful.

MALE CHARACTERISTICS
The influence of the yang force could result in the male Rat on the Roof facing a hard life, and he may have difficulties in sustaining a committed relationship. To guard against possible problems, he should always try to be in firm control of his inner energies, for otherwise they could become disruptive.

FAMILY AND FRIENDS
Your circle of friends consists of people who are similar to you. They enjoy your energy and are unthreatened by your forceful, dynamic personality.

Your family is another matter, however. They have had to live with your selfish demands and lack of consideration, and may have found you irritating, immature, or even simply rude. You are always likely to find little sympathy from your family unless you learn to vastly improve your general behavior.

RAT IN THE FIELD

~ 1936 1996 ~

*You live where the Rat finds life hard, but not impossible.
Out in the field, you can take whatever is available. You
show courage in all your actions.*

You go out and seek your fortune when others would stay at home and wait for better times. Sometimes you are tempted to take risks.

You are linked to a fire burning in the hearth. Properly controlled, you can offer companionship and warmth, but often you are a danger. You can blaze out of control and hurt those around you. Yet, with a little self-discipline, you can turn from scorching heat to warming fire, and from danger to comfort.

PERSONALITY
Your Rat nature surfaces most powerfully in your impatience and your temper. Combined with the excesses of youth, your temper suggests danger to yourself and also to others. It is likely, therefore, that your youth was problematic. However, you are also linked to summer, and as you get older, you

will find that it is easier to balance the forces within you, make the most of all situations, and apply your intelligence to your advantage.

Any Rats born in these years should never mistake their bravery for intelligence. You will always be tempted to put yourself into impossible situations, but you must try to be calm and rational. If this proves impossible, then make the most of what comes your way.

FEMALE CHARACTERISTICS
The fiery element within a female Rat in the Field is dangerous. Despite the calming yin influence, the fiery element could destroy the love and affection that her family hold for her.

MALE CHARACTERISTICS
The male Rat in the Field has none of these worries, however, and was born in a fortunate year.

Rat in the Field

EDUCATION

When you were young, it is likely that you were denied the best education. Luckily, this should cause no lasting problem for you – your innate Rat cunning and ability to plan, work, and eventually succeed should more than compensate for this early disadvantage.

RELATIONSHIPS

The passions you bring to any relationship will be intense, but your impatience and the heat of your passion could destroy what you love and revere the most. Take care, and tread a careful line between the strength of your emotions and the needs and feelings of others.

RAT IN THE WAREHOUSE

~ 1948 2008 ~

You are where every Rat wants to be — you have found the best position, and life is easy. You also have the opportunity to make the best of all situations.

You are a skillful Rat. You use your knowledge to your best advantage and should reap many rewards.

You are linked to a hand holding a reaping stick, or a flowering plant. Both of these symbols represent flourishing and plenty, which are likely to be yours if you are sensible.

FEMALE CHARACTERISTICS
Because of the yin influence, the female Rat in the Warehouse is likely to be pleasant, kind, and amenable, and should enjoy her life.

MALE CHARACTERISTICS
The male, however, has to cope with the yang influence, and is consquently prone to try much too hard to achieve more and more. It is advisable for the male to learn to relax and cultivate friendships, and not to allow them to be spoiled by selfishness or ambition.

FRIENDSHIPS
You may sometimes exhibit the unpleasant Rat tendency of being calculating and mean. Try not to let it happen if you possibly can. Remember that you can easily run into hard times when the warehouse is empty, and may have to ask your friends for sustenance and support.

RELATIONSHIPS
You are invariably comfortable and secure in your sense of self, and should be able to sustain good relationships. You are likely to have a healthy relationship with your partner, but you may experience difficulties with your children and may even find them irritating.

Perhaps this is because you have always found life to be easy. You are likely to feel that your children should earn their own way in the world and that if only they tried a

Rat in the Warehouse

little bit harder, then they could also enjoy a life as good and comfortable as yours. Your common sense and a touch of humility should help you to overcome such smugness.

PROSPECTS
Any Rats born in these years should try to control their calculating tendency. It is very important for you to realize when you are comfortable and happy. There will always be people who seem to have more than you, so do not be jealous. At the same time, do not despise those who seem to have less than you. Material benefits are very important to you, but you should strive to value your relationships and friendships just as highly.

RAT ON THE BEAM

~ 1900 1960 ~

*As the Rat on the Beam you are the kingpin — you have the
run of the house and little to fear. Many people depend
upon you for your vital support.*

The Chinese regard the beam as the mainstay of the home. It is the chief support of the whole house and is given considerable attention when a house is being built. Consequently, you are a very important Rat.

You are associated with the strength of gold and the wisdom gained by age. This strength, combined with wisdom, is likely to result in people perceiving you as someone who can be leaned upon in difficult times.

PERSONALITY
Over the years, you are likely to have learned to master the Rat's instinctive cunning and distrust. In their place, you should try to develop your innate intelligence and strengths, and you are fortunate to have both in substantial quantities. Try not to over-exert yourself during the quest for achievement and

success. Bear in mind that you are associated with wisdom and gold. This means that in the same way that gold can be continually refined, and wisdom is gained by experience, so your personality will naturally develop over a period of time.

FRIENDSHIPS
Your qualities will invariably ensure that you are powerful and fortunate, yet you will also gain people's true friendship and admiration.

You are popular, and other people consider you to be a sincere and trustworthy friend. You are likely to always be successful in your work, and indeed, in anything that you have decided to try your hand at.

FEMALE CHARACTERISTICS
The female Rat on the Beam is a highly talented woman. The influence of the yin force is likely to

Rat on the Beam

lead to her being respected. She should be particularly skillful at exerting control over events.

PROSPECTS

Sometimes you may feel that you have not been successful. This sense of failure should not be taken seriously, for you are likely to benefit from the good fortune that you have brought to others. Your innate drive to succeed is at the core of your personality, but try to remember that benefit does not always have to be in material terms.

Perhaps the love and support of your friends is the way in which you are blessed. If this is the case, you should not treat this blessing lightly. Only a fool equates success with material gains and achievements. As your wisdom invariably increases over the years, you are more likely to see that this is true.

RAT ON THE MOUNTAIN

~ 1912 1972 ~

*A Rat on the Mountain has traveled far away from its
natural environment. Consequently it is tired and fearful
and can find neither food nor shelter.*

You are linked to a man carrying a load upon his back, signifying fatigue and struggle. You are also associated with decline and the dead of winter. Even the natural vitality of the Rat seems unable to rise above this heavy and oppressive burden.

PERSONALITY

Many Rats born in these years find it difficult to be still and rest for too long, because they are usually constantly worried about what the future might bring.

Perhaps you often feel ill at ease and worry that you do not fit in among your peers or your friends. You may also fear that your achievements – invariably gained through your own hard work against considerable odds – are not going to last for long. Quite simply, all you have to do is acknowledge your position in life and enjoy being there.

This is difficult for most Rats on the Mountain, and unfortunately you seem to be driven by your fear.

The Rat's innate distrust of others is so highly developed in you that it could even have a detrimental effect on your life. Try not to be too worried and preoccupied about the future; and concentrate on the present instead.

FEMALE CHARACTERISTICS

The calming and soothing influence of the yin force should help the female Rat on the Mountain deal with the majority of her fears, but she is still likely to experience some emotional stress.

MALE CHARACTERISTICS

The male can sometimes be over-anxious, but if he takes care in his choice of partner, this should help him considerably.

Rat on the Mountain

YOUTH

When you were young, life may have seemed to be a struggle. Your education, family, relationships, and the early stages of your career are likely to cause you problems, but should all improve eventually.

RELATIONSHIPS

It is important for you to remember that the key to successful emotional relationships lies within your own personality. If you are untrusting, you will probably have to endure fearful and painful relationships. Learn to relax and trust your partner instead, and you should be able to enjoy a long and happy relationship.

PROSPECTS

Your prospects improve as you mature – by the time you reach your middle age, you should be able to enjoy your life much more. You are likely to reach a plateau of stability where you can relax and rest.

YOUR CHINESE
MONTH OF BIRTH

*Find the table with your year of birth, and see where your
birthday falls. For example, if you were born on
August 30, 1948, you were born in Chinese month 7.*

1 You were born very close to the
Year of the Pig. As a result, you are
calm and popular.

2 You have the potential to be very
successful, but must learn to control
your ego.

3 You appear to be confident, but
are actually insecure. You tend to
have an eventful emotional life.

4 You are trustworthy and
dependable, and have a flamboyant
aspect to your personality, too.

5 You are honest, trustworthy,
and naturally charming. As a result,
you make friends easily.

6 You are a natural extrovert. Try
to control your generosity, and
forgive your partner's faults.

7 You value your independence
and never stay anywhere for long.
Do not expect financial rewards.

8 You are adaptable, quick, and
very talented. You like an element of
risk and should be fortunate.

9 You are quiet, determined, and
not very adventurous. You find it
difficult to make close friends.

10 You are alert, persuasive, and
very talented. Some people might be
jealous of you, so be careful.

11 You are very blunt and a natural
leader. Remember that the best
leaders always listen to advice.

12 You are intelligent, creative, and
forceful. You can be fickle and should
try to control this trait.

* Some Chinese years contain double months:	
1900: Month 8	1936: Month 3
Aug 25 – Sept 23	March 23 – April 20
Sept 24 – Oct 22	April 21 – May 20
1960: Month 6	1984: Month 10
June 24 – July 23	Oct 24 – Nov 22
July 24 – Aug 21	Nov 23 – Dec 21

1900	
Jan 31 – Feb 29	1
March 1 – March 30	2
March 31 – April 28	3
April 2 – May 27	4
May 28 – June 26	5
June 2 – July 25	6
July 26 – Aug 24	7
See double months box	8
Oct 23 – Nov 21	9
Nov 22 – Dec 21	10
Dec 22 – Jan 19 1901	11
Jan 20 – Feb 18 1901	12

1912	
Feb 18 – March 18	1
March 19 – April 16	2
April 17 – May 16	3
May 17 – June 14	4
June 15 – Jul 13	5
July 14 – Aug 12	6
Aug 13 – Sept 10	7
Sept 11 – Oct 9	8
Oct 10 – Nov 8	9
Nov 9 – Dec 8	10
Dec 9 – Jan 6 1913	11
Jan 7 – Feb 5	12

1924	
Feb 5 – March 4	1
March 5 – April 3	2
April 4 – May 3	3
May 4 – June 1	4
June 2 – July 1	5
July 2 – July 31	6
Aug 1 – Aug 29	7
Aug 30 – Sept 28	8
Sept 29 – Oct 27	9
Oct 28 – Nov 26	10
Nov 27 – Dec 25	11
Dec 26 – Jan 23 1925	12

1936	
Jan 24 – Feb 22	1
Feb 23 – March 22	2
See double months box	3
May 21 – June 18	4
June 19 – July 17	5
July 18 – Aug 16	6
Aug 17 – Sept 15	7
Sept 16 – Oct 14	8
Oct 15 – Nov 13	9
Nov 14 – Dec 13	10
Dec 14 – Jan 12 1937	11
Jan 13 – Feb 10	12

1948	
Feb 10 – March 10	1
March 11 – April 8	2
April 9 – May 8	3
May 9 – June 6	4
June 7 – July 6	5
July 7 – Aug 4	6
Aug 5 – Sept 2	7
Sept 3 – Oct 2	8
Oct 3 – Oct 31	9
Nov 1 – Nov 30	10
Dec 1 – Dec 29	11
Dec 30 – Jan 28 1949	12

1960	
Jan 28 – Feb 26	1
Feb 27 – March 26	2
March 27 – April 25	3
April 26 – May 24	4
May 25 – June 23	5
See double months box	6
Aug 22 – Sept 20	7
Sept 21 – Oct 19	8
Oct 20 – Nov 18	9
Nov 19 – Dec 17	10
Dec 18 – Jan 16 1961	11
Jan 17 – Feb 14	12

1972	
Feb 15 – March 14	1
March 15 – April 13	2
April 14 – May 12	3
May 13 – June 10	4
June 11 – July 10	5
July 11 – Aug 8	6
Aug 9 – Sept 7	7
Sept 8 – Oct 6	8
Oct 7 – Nov 5	9
Nov 6 – Dec 5	10
Dec 6 – Jan 3 1973	11
Jan 4 – Feb 2	12

1984	
Feb 2 – March 2	1
March 3 – March 30	2
April 1 – April 30	3
May 1 – May 30	4
May 31 – June 28	5
June 29 – July 27	6
July 28 – Aug 26	7
Aug 27 – Sept 24	8
Sept 25 – Oct 23	9
See double months box	10
Dec 22 – Jan 20 1985	11
Jan 21 – Feb 19	12

1996	
Feb 19 – March 18	1
March 19 – April 17	2
April 18 – May 16	3
May 17 – June 15	4
June 16 – July 15	5
July 16 – Aug 13	6
Aug 14 – Sept 12	7
Sept 13 – Oct 11	8
Oct 12 – Nov 10	9
Nov 11 – Dec 10	10
Dec 11 – Jan 8 1997	11
Jan 9 – Feb 6	12

YOUR CHINESE
DAY OF BIRTH

*Refer to the previous page to discover the beginning of your
Chinese month of birth, then use the chart below to
calculate your Chinese day of birth.*

If you were born on May 5, 1900,
your birthday is in the month starting
on April 29. Find 29 on the chart
below. Using 29 as the first day,
count the days until you reach the
date of your birthday. (Remember
that not all months contain 31 days.)
You were born on day 7 of the
Chinese month.

If you were born in a Chinese
double month, simply count the days
from the first date of the month that
contains your birthday.

1	2	3	4	5	6	7
8	9	10	11	12	13	14
15	16	17	18	19	20	21
22	23	24	25	26	27	28
29	30	31				

DAY 1, 10, 19, OR 28
You are trustworthy and set high
standards, but tend to rush your

projects. Try to be cautious, and do
not be too self-obsessed. You may
receive unexpected money but must
control your spending. You are
suited to a career in the public sector
or the arts.

DAY 2, 11, 20, OR 29
You are honest and popular. You
need peace, but also require lively
company. You are prone to
outbursts of temper. You tend to
enjoy life and make the most of your
opportunities. You are suited to a
literary or artistic career.

DAY 3, 12, 21, OR 30
You are quick-witted, but may
appear to be difficult. As a result,
people may be wary of being your
friend. You have a disciplined
character and fight for the truth. You
are suited to careers that have a
competitive element.

Day 4, 13, 22, or 31

You are very warmhearted, but also have a reserved attitude, which can sometimes make you appear unapproachable. If you try to be more outgoing and sociable, you should become more popular. You have a calm and patient manner, and are suited to a career as an academic or researcher.

Day 5, 14, or 23

Your fiery, obstinate nature can sometimes make it difficult for you to accept suggestions or opinions from others, and your stubbornness may lead to quarrels or problems. You should be lucky with money and may often use your profits to set up new projects. Your innate intelligence will enable you to cope with a demanding career.

Day 6, 15, or 24

You have an open, stable, and cheerful character, and enjoy an active social life. You are affectionate and emotional, and have a tendency to daydream. This can lead to confusion, and your eagerness to help others may be stifled by your indecision. Although you will never be wealthy, you should always have enough money.

Day 7, 16, or 25

You enjoy a certain amount of excitement in your life, but must learn to become more realistic and disciplined. Although you are a natural performer, you should beware of alienating your friends or colleagues. In your career, the opportunity to travel is more important to you than a good salary or a high standard of living.

Day 8, 17, or 26

You have very good judgment, but should not act too quickly. Your social skills may sometimes be lacking, and you may alienate other people, so try to be more tactful. You will experience poverty, but also wealth. Your calm and determined nature is combined with a free spirit, making you best suited to self-employment.

Day 9, 18, or 27

You are happy, optimistic, and warmhearted. You keep yourself busy and are rarely troubled by trivialities. Occasionally you quarrel unnecessarily with your friends, and it is important for you to learn to control your moods. You are particularly suited to a career as a sole owner or proprietor.

YOUR CHINESE HOUR OF BIRTH

In Chinese time, one hour is equal to two Western hours. Each Chinese double hour is associated with one of the twelve astrological animals.

11 P.M. – 1 A.M. RAT HOUR
You are independent and have a hot temper. Try to think before you speak. Your thrifty nature will be useful in business and at home. You are willing to help those who are close to you, and they will return your support.

1 – 3 A.M. OX HOUR
Up to the age of twenty, your life could be difficult, but your fortunes are likely to improve after these troublesome years. In your career, be prepared to take a risk or to leave home during your youth to achieve your goals. You should enjoy a prosperous old age.

3 – 5 A.M. TIGER HOUR
You have a lively and creative nature, which may cause family arguments in your youth. Between the ages of twenty and forty you may have many problems. Luckily, your fortunes are likely to improve dramatically in your forties.

5 – 7 A.M. RABBIT HOUR
Your parents should be helpful, but your siblings may be your rivals. You may have to move away from home to achieve your full potential at work. Your committed relationship may take time to become settled, but you should get along much better with everyone after middle age.

7 – 9 A.M. DRAGON HOUR
You have a quick-witted, determined, and attractive nature. Your life will be busy, but you could sometimes be lonely. You should achieve a good standard of living. Try to curb your excessive self-confidence, for it could make working relationships difficult.

9 – 11 A.M. SNAKE HOUR

You have a talent for business and should find it easy to build your career and provide for your family. You have a very generous spirit and will gladly help your friends when they are in trouble. Unfortunately, family relationships are unlikely to run smoothly.

11 A.M. – 1 P.M. HORSE HOUR

You are active, clever, and obstinate. Try to listen to advice. You are fascinated with travel and with changing your life. Learn to control your extravagance, for it could lead to financial suffering.

1 – 3 P.M. RAM HOUR

Steady relationships with your family, friends, or partners are difficult, because you have an active nature. You are clever, but must not force your views on others. Your fortunes will be at their lowest in your middle age.

3 – 5 P.M. MONKEY HOUR

You earn and spend money easily. Your character is attractive, but frustrating, too. Sometimes your parents are not able to give you adequate moral support. Your committed relationship should be good, but do not brood over emotional problems for too long – if you do your career could suffer.

5 – 7 P.M. ROOSTER HOUR

In your teenage years you may have many arguments with your family. There could even be a family division, which should eventually be resolved. You are trustworthy, kind, and warmhearted, and never intend to hurt other people.

7 – 9 P.M. DOG HOUR

Your brave, capable, hard-working nature is ideally suited to self-employment, and the forecast for your career is excellent. Try to control your impatience and vanity. The quality of your life is far more important to you than the amount of money you have saved.

9 – 11 P.M. PIG HOUR

You are particularly skilled at manual work and always set yourself high standards. Although you are warmhearted, you do not like to surround yourself with too many friends. However, the people who are close to you have your complete trust. You can be easily upset by others, but are able to forgive and forget quickly.

YOUR FORTUNE IN OTHER ANIMAL YEARS

The Rat's fortunes fluctuate during the twelve animal years. It is best to concentrate on a year's positive aspects, and to take care when faced with the seemingly negative.

YEAR OF THE RAT
This is a mixed year for the Rat, though it is your own year. Your commercial life and any business transactions will be difficult, and unfortunately you are at risk. Do not despair, however, for luckily, the Chinese gods will protect you.

YEAR OF THE OX
This year is not an auspicious time for the Rat. Although you will enjoy yourself immensely in the social area of your life, your income will diminish, and you will find that your work becomes both stressful and difficult.

YEAR OF THE TIGER
Life tends to go very smoothly indeed for the Rat during the Year of the Tiger. You should be able to achieve considerable success in your career or profession, while enjoying your social life to the fullest.

YEAR OF THE RABBIT
Fortune smiles on you throughout this year, and it should prove to be one of your very best. You will enjoy success in your family life, in your social relationships, and in your professional life. Try your hardest to make the most of everything.

YEAR OF THE DRAGON
This is potentially a good year for the Rat, and promotion and success are likely to be yours. Make sure, however, that you are sufficiently quick to seize opportunities while they last, and be prepared to take on new areas of responsibility.

YEAR OF THE SNAKE

Although this year will open with opportunity, unfortunately this same opportunity can also eventually lead to failure and financial distress. There is a possibility that you will suffer a bereavement in your family during this year.

YEAR OF THE HORSE

Be warned – this year is a dangerous time for you, because you are particularly susceptible to accidents. Consequently, you must take great care throughout the Year of the Horse and should not act without considering the risks involved.

YEAR OF THE RAM

This is a year of mixed fortunes for the Rat. Promotion should be yours, but it would be a mistake to think that good fortune is going to be with you throughout the year, because accidents are also likely to rear their heads.

YEAR OF THE MONKEY

Someone you know is likely to die this year, but they will leave you money or property. The result of this bequest will be increased independence, but you are likely to find that this new independence also brings conflict into your life.

YEAR OF THE ROOSTER

Try to prepare yourself for various disagreements that could escalate into legal proceedings. It may seem unfair, but all your conscientiousness and diligence during this year are likely to be relatively unrewarded.

YEAR OF THE DOG

Unfortunately, the Year of the Dog is not an auspicious year for the Rat. There is nothing you can do about it, so you may as well learn to accept that you will feel bemused, bewildered, and generally out of sorts throughout this year.

YEAR OF THE PIG

At first, it may seem as if last year's misfortune is happening all over again – nothing seems to work right and all your plans get delayed. Do not despair, however, for more successful times are definitely on the horizon.

YOUR CHINESE
YEAR OF BIRTH

*Your astrological animal corresponds to the Chinese year of
your birth. It is the single most important key in the quest
to unlock your Chinese horoscope.*

Find your Western year of birth in the left-hand column of the chart. Your Chinese astrological animal is on the same line as your year of birth in the right-hand column of the chart. If you were born in the beginning of the year, check the

middle column of the chart carefully. For example, if you were born in 1961, you might assume that you belong to the Year of the Ox. However, if your birthday falls before February 15, you actually belong to the Year of the Rat.

1900	Jan 31 – Feb 18, 1901	Rat
1901	Feb 19 – Feb 7, 1902	Ox
1902	Feb 8 – Jan 28, 1903	Tiger
1903	Jan 29 – Feb 15, 1904	Rabbit
1904	Feb 16 – Feb 3, 1905	Dragon
1905	Feb 4 – Jan 24, 1906	Snake
1906	Jan 25 – Feb 12, 1907	Horse
1907	Feb 13 – Feb 1, 1908	Ram
1908	Feb 2 – Jan 21, 1909	Monkey
1909	Jan 22 – Feb 9, 1910	Rooster
1910	Feb 10 – Jan 29, 1911	Dog
1911	Jan 30 – Feb 17, 1912	Pig
1912	Feb 18 – Feb 5, 1913	Rat
1913	Feb 6 – Jan 25, 1914	Ox
1914	Jan 26 – Feb 13, 1915	Tiger
1915	Feb 14 – Feb 2, 1916	Rabbit
1916	Feb 3 – Jan 22, 1917	Dragon

1917	Jan 23 – Feb 10, 1918	Snake
1918	Feb 11 – Jan 31, 1919	Horse
1919	Feb 1 – Feb 19, 1920	Ram
1920	Feb 20 – Feb 7, 1921	Monkey
1921	Feb 8 – Jan 27, 1922	Rooster
1922	Jan 28 – Feb 15, 1923	Dog
1923	Feb 16 – Feb 4, 1924	Pig
1924	Feb 5 – Jan 23, 1925	Rat
1925	Jan 24 – Feb 12, 1926	Ox
1926	Feb 13 – Feb 1, 1927	Tiger
1927	Feb 2 – Jan 22, 1928	Rabbit
1928	Jan 23 – Feb 9, 1929	Dragon
1929	Feb 10 – Jan 29, 1930	Snake
1930	Jan 30 – Feb 16, 1931	Horse
1931	Feb 17 – Feb 5, 1932	Ram
1932	Feb 6 – Jan 25, 1933	Monkey
1933	Jan 26 – Feb 13, 1934	Rooster

1934	Feb 14 – Feb 3, 1935	Dog	1971	Jan 27 – Feb 14, 1972	Pig
1935	Feb 4 – Jan 23, 1936	Pig	1972	Feb 15 – Feb 2, 1973	Rat
1936	Jan 24 – Feb 10, 1937	Rat	1973	Feb 3 – Jan 22, 1974	Ox
1937	Feb 11 – Jan 30, 1938	Ox	1974	Jan 23 – Feb 10, 1975	Tiger
1938	Jan 31 – Feb 18, 1939	Tiger	1975	Feb 11 – Jan 30, 1976	Rabbit
1939	Feb 19 – Feb 7, 1940	Rabbit	1976	Jan 31 – Feb 17, 1977	Dragon
1940	Feb 8 – Jan 26, 1941	Dragon	1977	Feb 18 – Feb 6, 1978	Snake
1941	Jan 27 – Feb 14, 1942	Snake	1978	Feb 7 – Jan 27, 1979	Horse
1942	Feb 15 – Feb 4, 1943	Horse	1979	Jan 28 – Feb 15, 1980	Ram
1943	Feb 5 – Jan 24, 1944	Ram	1980	Feb 16 – Feb 4, 1981	Monkey
1944	Jan 25 – Feb 12, 1945	Monkey	1981	Feb 5 – Jan 24, 1982	Rooster
1945	Feb 13 – Feb 1, 1946	Rooster	1982	Jan 25 – Feb 12, 1983	Dog
1946	Feb 2 – Jan 21, 1947	Dog	1983	Feb 13 – Feb 1, 1984	Pig
1947	Jan 22 – Feb 9, 1948	Pig	1984	Feb 2 – Feb 19, 1985	Rat
1948	Feb 10 – Jan 28, 1949	Rat	1985	Feb 20 – Feb 8, 1986	Ox
1949	Jan 29 – Feb 16, 1950	Ox	1986	Feb 9 – Jan 28, 1987	Tiger
1950	Feb 17 – Feb 5, 1951	Tiger	1987	Jan 29 – Feb 16, 1988	Rabbit
1951	Feb 6 – Jan 26, 1952	Rabbit	1988	Feb 17 – Feb 5, 1989	Dragon
1952	Jan 27 – Feb 13, 1953	Dragon	1989	Feb 6 – Jan 26, 1990	Snake
1953	Feb 14 – Feb 2, 1954	Snake	1990	Jan 27 – Feb 14, 1991	Horse
1954	Feb 3 – Jan 23, 1955	Horse	1991	Feb 15 – Feb 3, 1992	Ram
1955	Jan 24 – Feb 11, 1956	Ram	1992	Feb 4 – Jan 22, 1993	Monkey
1956	Feb 12 – Jan 30, 1957	Monkey	1993	Jan 23 – Feb 9, 1994	Rooster
1957	Jan 31 – Feb 17, 1958	Rooster	1994	Feb 10 – Jan 30, 1995	Dog
1958	Feb 18 – Feb 7, 1959	Dog	1995	Jan 31 – Feb 18, 1996	Pig
1959	Feb 8 – Jan 27, 1960	Pig	1996	Feb 19 – Feb 6, 1997	Rat
1960	Jan 28 – Feb 14, 1961	Rat	1997	Feb 7 – Jan 27, 1998	Ox
1961	Feb 15 – Feb 4, 1962	Ox	1998	Jan 28 – Feb 15, 1999	Tiger
1962	Feb 5 – Jan 24, 1963	Tiger	1999	Feb 16 – Feb 4, 2000	Rabbit
1963	Jan 25 – Feb 12, 1964	Rabbit	2000	Feb 5 – Jan 23, 2001	Dragon
1964	Feb 13 – Feb 1, 1965	Dragon	2001	Jan 24 – Feb 11, 2002	Snake
1965	Feb 2 – Jan 20, 1966	Snake	2002	Feb 12 – Jan 31, 2003	Horse
1966	Jan 21 – Feb 8, 1967	Horse	2003	Feb 1 – Jan 21, 2004	Ram
1967	Feb 9 – Jan 29, 1968	Ram	2004	Jan 22 – Feb 8, 2005	Monkey
1968	Jan 30 – Feb 16, 1969	Monkey	2005	Feb 9 – Jan 28, 2006	Rooster
1969	Feb 17 – Feb 5, 1970	Rooster	2006	Jan 29 – Feb 17, 2007	Dog
1970	Feb 6 – Jan 26, 1971	Dog	2007	Feb 18 – Feb 6, 2008	Pig